# Praise for *The Long Defeat*

T0300796

"Drawing from a place of isolation, loss, and despair, Patrick Connors navigates mundane alienation of contemporary survival with resolute grace. He leads his readers out of collective uncertainty towards the light of a better tomorrow, displaying an inner peace earned through perseverance. *The Long Defeat* is this poet's best work."

— **Brandon Pitts**
author of *Tender in the Age of Fury* and
*Pressure to Sing*

"An antithesis to defeat, this poetry collection is a testament of the human spirit's hard-earned victory over life's decohering forces. Patrick Connors' words are doorways from our everyday moments into the deeper awareness and magic of stillness and presence."

— **Josie Di Sciascio-Andrews**
author of seven collections of poetry and
two non-fiction books

"Patrick Connors' poetry collection, *The Long Defeat*, is in a powerful and descriptive voice that exposes his compassionate side and his descriptive ability. He speaks candidly of having experienced aloneness, despair, and regrets, though his faith remained strong. It is clear that Patrick Connors has lived *The Long Defeat* and is scarred, though his eye, his heart, and his hands create work that speaks with the courageous authority of a beautiful soul."

— **Bernadette Gabay Dyer**
author of four novels, two short story collections,
and a poetry collection

"The poems in *The Long Defeat* sing of the profound triumphs of the undefeated and of the undefeatable human spirit. When Connors writes, 'I have not been overcome ... and that will have to do for now,' the reader might take consolation in that strength of character and in such companionship as these poems provide between writer and reader."

— **John B. Lee**
Poet Laureate of Brantford, ON, and the
Canada Caribbean Literary Alliance

"An old friend of mine once shared with me that she loved Blues because it was a music that expressed a sadness that we can all connect to. In his poetic opus, *The Long Defeat*, Connors is writing the Blues. These are poems that express all of our traumas, fears, feelings of isolation, and sadness with thought-filled, relatable verse."

— **Dane Swan**
Finalist, 2017 Trillium Book Prize for Poetry, and
editor of *Changing the Face of Canadian Literature*

"Through heartfelt testaments to loss and hopefulness, *The Long Defeat* delves passionately into a shoreline meditation on 'failure' triumph, and 'isolation . . . between his burning toes' [and features] Connors' signature candour and generous self-examining wit."

— **David Bateman**
spoken word poet with four collections of poetry

"Clear as the headwaters of a fierce river, *The Long Defeat* is a collection about conquest and mastery, revealing in flashes, the many faces of a man's war with the world and himself. It's a book of small triumphs and, in the end, a huge victory."

— **Sabyaschi (Sachi) Nag**
author of three collections of poetry, including
*Could You Please Stop Singing?*

*Continued on page 85…*

# The Long Defeat

# The Long Defeat

Poems by
## Patrick Connors

Library and Archives Canada Cataloguing in Publication

Title: The long defeat / poems by Patrick Connors.

Names: Connors, Patrick, 1969- author.

Identifiers: Canadiana (print) 20240304993
Canadiana (ebook) 20240305019

ISBN 9781771617642 (softcover) | ISBN 9781771617666 (EPUB)
ISBN 9781771617659 (PDF) | ISBN 9781771617673 (Kindle)

Subjects: LCGFT: Poetry.

Classification: LCC PS8605.O566 L66 2024
DDC C811/.6—dc23

Published by Mosaic Press, Oakville, Ontario, Canada, 2024.
MOSAIC PRESS, Publishers
www.Mosaic-Press.com
Copyright © Patrick Connors 2024

Cover Photo: "Winter Road" by Rosemary Komori. This photo was the inspiration
for the poem, "Country Road" on page 62.

All rights reserved. Without limiting the rights under copyright reserved here, no
part of this publication may be reproduced, stored in or introduced into any retrieval
system, or transmitted in any form or by any means—electronic, mechanical,
by photocopy, recording or otherwise—without the prior written permission and
consent of both the copyright owners and the Publisher of this book.

Printed and bound in Canada.

ONTARIO ARTS COUNCIL
CONSEIL DES ARTS DE L'ONTARIO
an Ontario government agency
un organisme du gouvernement de l'Ontario

Funded by the Government of Canada
Financé par le gouvernement du Canada

ONTARIO CREATES

MOSAIC PRESS
1252 Speers Road, Units 1 & 2, Oakville, Ontario, L6L 2X4 (905) 825-2130
info@mosaic-press.com • www.mosaic-press.com

*In Memory of Mick Burrs,*
*who helped me become*
*a better poet and a better person*

# Table of Contents

The Long Defeat that Brings Us What We Know.................................1

Becoming .................................................................................2

Prisoner ..................................................................................3

Toil..........................................................................................4

A Period of Transition...............................................................5

Hemispheres............................................................................7

Moments in Time .....................................................................8

The New Normal.......................................................................9

Our Road ...............................................................................10

Virus......................................................................................11

Vacation.................................................................................12

Aphorisms of the CoronApocalypse..........................................13

Voices ....................................................................................15

The World is on Fire ...............................................................17

Hope......................................................................................18

Eternal...................................................................................19

Violet.....................................................................................20

New........................................................................................21

40 Days..................................................................................22

Ode to my Dad........................................................................23

Finding Myself........................................................................25

Bad Poem About Aging ...........................................................27

Good Brains ...........................................................................28

Aspire ....................................................................................29

All I Have to Do is Write..........................................................30

Calling....................................................................................31

Various Short Poems ...............................................................33

The Day Before Canada Day.................................................................35

North................................................................................................36

The Day After Canada Day..............................................................37

Simcoe Day.....................................................................................38

Poutine............................................................................................40

#RAPTORS....................................................................................41

Advent.............................................................................................42

Scars................................................................................................43

Kingston Road in the 1980's...........................................................44

Again...............................................................................................45

Wire.................................................................................................46

Juice.................................................................................................47

Center..............................................................................................48

Spiritual Warfare..........................................................................,.49

In My Own Words..........................................................................51

The Real Stuff.................................................................................52

Middle-Aged White Men Are Ruining the World...........................54

All I Could Get Down.....................................................................55

The Path..........................................................................................56

Big Time..........................................................................................57

What I Do for a Living....................................................................58

Try...................................................................................................59

Lead with Love................................................................................61

Country Road...................................................................................62

Down Time......................................................................................63

Pantoum..........................................................................................64

Trust................................................................................................65

Darkness..........................................................................................66

A Matter of Faith............................................................................68

Micah...............................................................................................69

Ecumenism.......................................................................................71

The Day of my Dad's Memorial ................................................................ 72
After Four of Us Have Been Let Go ........................................................ 75
Supper ................................................................................................... 77

Acknowledgments .................................................................................. 79
Some Notes on Prior Publication ............................................................ 81

"The most beautiful people we have known are those who have known defeat, known suffering, known struggle, known loss, and have found their way out of the depths. These persons have an appreciation, a sensitivity, and an understanding of life that fills them with compassion, gentleness, and a deep loving concern. Beautiful people do not just happen."

— Elizabeth Kubler Ross

# The Long Defeat that Brings Us What We Know[*]

He loves the beach.
He walks barefoot along the shoreline
as close to the water without getting wet
while as far away from people as possible.

Like every man, he experiences
loss, failure, isolation, accusations
numerous as the grains of sand
between his burning toes.

The beach is where he finds peace.
It is his favourite place to pray
to the One who formed this beauty
as a gift to all who would receive it.

He prays for the world
which once again suffers so much.
He prays it will not be swept away
by rising tides of hatred.

He prays for his family
    he prays for his friends
        he prays for his enemies
he prays to be able to tell the difference.

He rests at the end of a concrete pier.
"I have not been overcome,"
he proclaims to the setting sun,
"and that will have to do for now."

---

[*]   The title is a line from the poem "Neruda, the Wine," by Muriel Rukeyser

# Becoming

*it is always becoming a poem*
*this furnace, this fire*
*in a corner of the body's dark*

*this is the place that burns*
*whatever has been broken*

"Heart," by Mick Burrs

The world says
we are the result
of the residue
it leaves upon us.

Don't let this be.
Burn this dross from me!
No matter the pain it brings
I will not be like everyone else.

Mould me in your image
form me in the refiner's crucible
that my thoughts, my work
and my poetry may bring you glory.

Let all the indescribable pain
endured while becoming understandable
bring clarity to my vision
and integrity to my life.

Then my words would blaze
a trail across the midnight sky
and be a likeness of the light
which will forever shut out darkness.

# Prisoner

I have lost my voice.
The only word I have ever felt beating
in my heart, echoing through my mind
has been taken from me.

The other prisoners
hiss and whisper the words
the broken-hearted cannot say out loud
and leave me in solitary silence.

But I know why.
They don't understand
the burden I am bound to carry
and must keep hidden deep inside.

This burden keeps me alive.
It gives me passion and purpose
and is the only thing I have
which is real.

If this word trapped in my throat
found daylight at the tip of my tongue
I would sing and shout, laugh and cry
and my sentence would be complete.

If I could see her again
make love to her slowly and gently
if I could say her name once more
then I would be free.

# Toil
*for Dane*

Blinded by beams of mind-numbing light
from a soulless, fluorescent sun
you begin another nameless day.

The air crackles bolts of static
buzzes and hums its monotone din
which makes hearing hard and hearts harder.

Surrounded by a sea of hope gone cold
you hold your breath and jump feet first
not knowing when you will hit ground.

You are a digger.
You trace a line with common courtesy
around basic humanity and then cut into it.

You dig, try to get below the surface.
The terrain is bare and unyielding
so you dig and you dig some more.

You are not sure of what you will find,
how to recognize the results of your work
if they are real or have any value to anyone.

# A Period of Transition
## *In Honour of O Puck*

March 21st.

The first full day of spring.
Birds are chirping, the sun shines
leaves are forming on the trees.

Today is the day
       O Puck has left this dimension.

And yet I know

               his spirit lives on.

He taught us in 2012
      that the end of the Mayan calendar
            was NOT

                  the end of the world

but merely a new beginning...

"The universe is in a period of transition," O Puck said,
"All the stars and planets
         are in perfect alignment.

"It has taken us over 5000 years
to get to this point, but make no mistake -
our time has come.

"If you are not ready for our destiny
               the world will leave you behind.

"But if you will accept this new dawning
　　　the importance of mother earth, the sacredness of all people

　　　　　　　then you are ready for the days
　　　　　　which will change the world forever."

I know I will see O Puck again
　　　after I have made my period of transition.

We will laugh and hug, and he will tell a joke
　　　about an angel, a poet
　　　　　　　and the eagle.

And we will laugh again
　　　and he will teach me how
　　　　　　　to live in a world beyond enlightenment.

# Hemispheres

My introvert side
is glad to actually have a rest:
Breathes, exhales slowly, sinks into his chair.

He sets priorities, contemplates, makes plans
yet accepts the folly of making plans –
releases all to its fulfillment.

My extrovert side
wants to eat sushi, drink draught beer
experience the world beyond his front door.

He cannot bear to stay inside
while there is an outside which must be changed.
In the distance a siren sounds, a call to action right now!

It doesn't matter
which side of my brain I would like to follow:
At least I have passed five minutes of the pandemic.

# Moments in Time

I am in lockdown
separated from society
trapped by a worldwide crisis
with an unknown outcome.

Eating and cleaning slowly lead
to the grey peak of the afternoon
when I am made dull and sullen
by anxiety and despair.

I go out to the yard
to see if fresh air and movement
will provide a sense of release
from uncertainty and boredom.

As I walk my solitary circle
I pass this moment in time
with nothing else to do
other than get through it.

I go back inside and take a nap
balance my checkbook, read a poem
watch a rerun of *M\*A\*S\*H* for the 400th time
and figure out how to pass the evening.

A late April rain washes out
the muddy tracks I left on the lawn
the one and only hour of sunlight
and the hope for a brighter tomorrow.

# The New Normal

The world reaps a harvest of desolation -
sickness and ruin are all around.

As you cocoon in the name of health
you grow obsessed by a cinema of thought.

You have nothing but time to rehearse
all you have ever said and done.

The director running the scene yells,
"Cut!", and you replay it from the top.

No matter how many takes
you just can't seem to get anything right.

Yet it is safer to stay in this nightmare
than to live the reality going on outside.

You are haunted by the past, terrified
of the present, and can't imagine a future.

Then comes the turning point -
you try to escape the trap you created.

But, just as you think you are free
the hellish screenplay loops in your mind.

Such is how you pass your hours.
And the hours become days.

The days become weeks, the weeks
become months, without any resolution.

# Our Road
*for Mrs. G.*

On sunny days
we strolled by the schoolyard
recalled our latest game
and talked trash to each other.

They say that life is what you make it.
One moment you're 15, the next you're 50.
The loss you have had is less than the love
you have gained until there is another loss.

On rainy days
we ran by the schoolyard
splashed little drops of happiness
which mixed sweetly with our tears.

Life is what it is today.
You share a meal made of love
and are afraid to take the leftovers
in case they might be the last.

# Virus

We are all having
the same nightmare, overcome
by an invisible, relentless enemy
completely unable to protect ourselves.

People are dying by the dozens
doing the work we take for granted.
Undervalued, often underpaid labour
suddenly something we can't live without.

People are dying alone
in soiled beds made up of despair.
They lie along walls wailing prayers
wishing they could say their last goodbyes.

# Vacation

Five days off work, but The Pandemic rages on.

I can't travel, seek new surroundings.
I can't go to a ballgame or concert.
I can't really leave the house. But
I must make the best of it.

I'm going to take a vacation
    from not being grateful
        for everything I have.
The alternative is becoming intolerable.

I'm going to take a vacation from bitterness.
I'm going to take the week off
from trying not to enjoy life
until I can change the world.

I'm going to take a vacation
from convincing everyone
that I am right or I am good
and not care too much what anyone thinks.

I suppose in a week I might feel better.

# Aphorisms of the CoronApocalypse
## *Things that I Know*

2020. The year of Covid-19.
That's how this will be remembered.

In twenty years or one hundred
after the next plague or disaster strikes.

In history books and documentaries
in Google searches and think tanks.

They will have the numbers of those who fell ill
bar graphs to tell how many of us died.

I will not be a statistic.
I will not be recalled as an item of data.

I have many things I need to accomplish
some of them important, I assure you.

But right now, they are all on hold
while I choose to stay inside.

When this siege ends
I know I will emerge with a greater vision.

I will be stronger and more capable
because waiting is not a passive exercise.

I will be clearer about my priorities.
I will live my life with more integrity.

I know we are fighting other plagues
which undermine the best we can be.

I pray there will be legal justice
for the hate crimes being committed.

I know I will strive for social justice
especially when they say it's impossible.

I know there are some who do not wish
the world as I see it to be fulfilled.

I know I will change the minds
of one or two if I continue to try.

I do believe it will get better
if we keep the flame of hope alive.

I know I will build up a community
of like-minded people; even if some won't like me.

I know that if we serve one another
we will serve the higher purpose.

I know we can beat the bastards
who want to divide and break us.

I know we can rewrite history
if only we have the courage.

I know that biblical-level pestilence
made me finally write this poem.

I believe we can be better when this ends.
I know I will be glad when it ends.

# Voices

The people speak power.
The revelation is being televised.
It fills your city streets
and it's in your living room!

A winter of discontent
and a spring of isolation
have us set for a summer
which will yield a harvest of change.

We are actors in an ongoing narrative
reaching a turning point of no return.
It's time for the truth to come out.

I am anti-fascist.
I'm not against the law.
I am not an anarchist.
And I am Pro-Christ!

For God's Sake, and our own
let's fight for reform. We can't
keep going on
                    the way things are.

When the people shout:
"BLACK LIVES MATTER!"
of course they mean
                    every life matters.

But, if anyone has to say,
"We Matter!", for this long
it means they are still being
treated like they don't matter!

Let anybody who takes a knee
with someone they never stood beside
be ready to confess their sins.

Let's have a first response which responds
in a way which gives us all value
and is protective of society.

Let them have proper training
to empathize with those suffering
a moment of crisis and a lifetime of adversity.

Let's not let
the military industrial complex
take away what is left of our freedom.

Let this be the time
we all bring our voices
to collectively name the never-forgotten.

Let's honour Lester Donaldson.
Let's honour Trayvon Martin.
Let's honour Breonna Taylor.
And not let it happen again.

# The World is On Fire
## *It's Hotter Than It's Ever Been*

British Columbia's forests are ablaze
burning centuries of growth
killing innocent animals
threatens the communities
the very fabric of the civilization
that produced the pollution
and caused the greenhouse gases
which raised the temperature of our planet.

The wind blows
plumes of acrid smoke
over the Rocky Mountains
across the Prairies
under the waterline
through the 6:00 news
blots the sky with ashen cover
that turns the setting sun into a dire warning.

California also burns, and Greece, too.
Catastrophic flooding in Africa and Europe
and New York and New Jersey, so-called
500-year events that are happening
with increased frequency.
Just when it seems it can't get worse,
Greenland's ice summit witnesses rain
for the first time in recorded history.

# Hope

In the season of planned fallow
Seeds I didn't plant or tend
Bore bitter fruit I had to eat
To keep me going but not thrive

The seeds I desire to plant
And tend for the rest of my days
Seem blown away by changing winds,
Or hidden by the year's first snow

Patient or not, time will always get
All that it needs for completion
So I settle in for the rest I need
And to make myself ready

Faith worth having grows because
Of powerful storms beyond control;
Shivering and shaken as I am, I await
The proving such tests shall bring

The hope of Spring is all I have
To keep me warm through this Winter
Which doesn't seem to have an end:
I will hold onto my hope

# Eternal

*"...and grace will lead me home."*
*Amazing Grace, John Newton*

Under grey November skies
which winter follows close behind

the leader of the free world
will not admit he lost the election

the premier of Ontario sacrifices
our health to feed the machine

and a 12-year-old boy out with his mother
is shot dead in gangster crossfire.

For the love of God, which we can't earn
we must resist the powers of darkness

until the end of their unfolding
becomes the beginning of true light.

In a world where a beautiful boy
paid for sins he didn't commit

let us hold him close in our hearts
and leave the rest to the Lord.

# Violet

One candle flickers in the cold dark
until it's time to light the second candle.

This is the season of preparation.
These are the middle times between
the promise and its fulfillment.

I will not get there
by having, by doing, or by getting –
only by rest and reflection.

I know I have been saved from myself.
I know there is hope for the future.
But I don't know what I have right now.

# New

Oh-one-oh-one twenty-twenty-one
the day we made sure 2020 hasn't won.

I woke up not quite right in the head
ready to shave last night off my tongue

unearth the mysteries of sweet gone bitter
wondering why I didn't expect this result.

The New Year has arrived
not fresh and clear as I would like

but neither am I.
I will try to find

the light of calm inside the
heavy darkness and go from there.

# 40 Days
*for the Scarborough Poetry Club*


It was the darkest winter in seventy-three years. Wiarton Willie didn't see his shadow
on February 2nd. The scientific precision of a groundhog weather forecast is difficult
to prove, yet something to consider. Friends said they expected an early spring.

But not me. Between my lack of physical mobility, the death of several friends,
and the disconnect between where my life is and where I thought it would be, I was trapped
in spiritual shackles which could not be unlocked by flipping the page of a calendar.

Then, it snowed. It snowed half a winter's worth in 10 days. The groundhog continued
his hibernation. And then, it snowed again. I sought shelter from the storms.

Under the cover of sunless days, in the self-absorption of bitterness, I found another
layer to explore, and digging through this brought me relief.

I discovered joy is not the realization of happiness. Joy is in the anticipation, the
expectation! By this belief we make it through the winter.

# Ode to my Dad
## *What I Am Left With*

Walter Gretzky died two days before my Dad.
They were both born in 1938. Other than that,
they had almost nothing in common.

My Dad and me also had very little in common
except our first names
and our last

the propensity to drink
as a means of dealing with anxiety
and a deep and abiding love in Jesus Christ.

My childhood was a hopeless struggle, founded
on pleasing my Dad, protecting my Mom
and becoming the next Wayne Gretzky.

My Dad was deeply damaged.
He was torn between trying to save us
from this damage and sharing how it felt.

Finally, we became
a family, found the courage
to leave the source of our abuse.

I started to live my life
and make my own mistakes
and then, eventually, become sane.

Decades later, after
a few vain attempts to make peace
I found out my Dad was very ill.

I couldn't go see him.
In the times of Covid, 5 provinces away
it just wasn't possible.

From decades gone by
the distance may as well have been
a million miles, even in the same room.

My Dad died.
The pain he felt and the pain he inflicted
cannot be reconciled.

I never got to tell him how much he hurt me.
I never got to say I forgave him.
I never got to say goodbye.

# Finding Myself

*Strive to change the world*
*in such a way that there's*
*no further need to be a dissident.*
Ferlinghetti, *Poetry as Insurgent Art*, page 8

Rising up from deep within
the very core of my being
the essence of who I am

underneath my public image
    is the need to find
someone to admire.

Lawrence Ferlinghetti spoke the words
the world needed to hear
at that exact moment.

Best of the Beats
because he promoted the rest
above himself.

Paragon of enlightenment
inspirer of a new way of being
artistic role model.

Ferlinghetti would have loathed
such titles based on what
little I know about him.

He would have frowned
if not downright sneered
at such fanboy foppery.

In the same way
many reading or hearing this could be offended
by words like humanist, socialist,

countercultural, malcontent, protestor,
activist, freethinker, nonconformist.

In the Coney Island of My Mind
- or, more accurately, Exhibition Place -
I get to play with words

turn image into meaning and back again
with enough musicality to form a poetry
of concise language and complex thought

imagine these words
making this world a better place
at least for a moment

and believe if I say them with clarity
and integrity for long enough
you may just listen to me.

# Bad Poem About Aging

The wrinkles under my eyes
are from unresolved attempts
to see the world in a different way.

I will never colour my hair –
it would probably make me look older,
and the chemicals could burn my scalp.

One of these days the spare tire
in my mid-section will disappear
with 50 crunches a day or prayer.

Or end up in the trunk
of the car I have never owned.

I am a telemarketer.
I sell pens and calendars and
other promotional products to Americans
who have total contempt for me, but want the stuff.

I die a little bit inside every time I don't get an order.
I die a little bit inside every time I do.

It is the only thing in this world for which I am qualified
other than to write poetry and hope for social justice.

One of these days this hope will become action.
The sleepy doldrums of middle-age shall
give way to new energy and life.

With wings like eagles, I will soar
on the wind that gave me breath and
spirit to carry me through these times.

# Good Brains
*for Charles and Neil*

This is the story of two men I would
emulate and aspire to be alike
while still being myself.

Their beautiful minds consumed by
a problematic quest for perfection
they have now finally found.

Charles Roach: The greatest man I have
ever known. He fought those who sought
to beat down freedom and did so with grace.

Neil Peart: The greatest drummer
I will ever know. There was depth and
poetry enough to fill his heart and hands.

These very different men had little
in common other than the desire
to move to their own unique rhythm

the propensity to inspire
and the genius ability to lead others
to the greatness they also could achieve.

I will follow my own vision of perfection -
or, at least as close to it as possible while
still a resident of this dimension.

If I can make this world a little better
transcend to what's above while within it
then I could be like Charles and Neil.

# Aspire

Humility.
Patience.
Wisdom.

I have read many books on the latter, listened to stories
of the connected as well as the down-and-out
and learned what I could from them.

I have only come this far by grace.
Decades of my life have passed with nothing
but promises and the knowledge they will be fulfilled.

King Solomon was probably the wisest man who ever lived.
He had wives and influence beyond the aspirations of ordinary men.
Most of his best writing came from a spirit of deep depression.

I will try to learn from these hard-won lessons
open my eyes and mind to the new day which dawns
when I realize the true beginning of my love.

# All I Have to Do is Write

Hemingway was overcome by his need
to be a metaphor for manhood.
Sylvia Plath endured misery, depression,

and Ted Hughes, until she could no more.
Dylan Thomas raged, debauched, and
womanized, until his light died.

Szymborska told us about having to clean up
after war. John McCrae wrote Canada's
greatest poem during World War I.

Joy Harjo became American
Poet Laureate describing the fallout
of the war they wage on her own people.

We are all at war on many fronts.
Some of it in the where we are, some
of it unresolved battles from years gone by.

Some of these wars we fight alone, others
in solidarity with a found community. Sometimes
it feels all is lost, but this usually precedes victory.

I am blessed and honoured to share my words,
to be part of an ongoing dialogue, to try and
make sense of the stuff of our lives.

# Calling
*After Pablo Neruda*


I was at that age
where a man from this society
should have a career, a car
a purpose clear to all around him.

Yet there was so much more I lacked –
integrity, passion, commitment.
I didn't have a public face, and I could
barely look at myself in the mirror.

Then, just as I had nearly accepted
a living death which aspired to mediocrity
my entire myopic world imploded
caved in by a gust of putrid wind.

I had a clear choice –
be destroyed by impure nonsense
embrace the abyss of a world
not worth being in

where I only occasionally
received guilty pleasure
and a sick sense of belonging –
or rejoin the path I had once followed.

Long had I ignored the summons.
I knew exactly where it came from –
pure wisdom patiently waited
until I finally answered her call.

I overcame the mere existence
I left behind, while being prepared
by repeated trials and refining fire
for the inspired life which will define me.

# Various Short Poems

### Out of My Own Words
*for Cricket*

Warming morning dew
rises up from fresh cut grass
a new beginning

### Food for Thought

The world
is a movable feast
which cannot satisfy

### Alone

Beneath the midnight moon
the waves of a lake flow gently
into the endless night.

### Blood

When love and pain
are so deep, it goes
on for generations.

### Burning Summer

all the way to Mount Pearl
smoke rises
from the forest fire

## Apocalypse Not

Sour taste of boredom
the pure sweetness of knowing
this is not the end

# The Day Before Canada Day

A young doe, more than a yearling,
pokes her head out between two trees
adjacent to the gate of the parking lot
in front of the building where I live.

The beautiful creature furtively climbs
a shallow hill leading to the sidewalk.
To her left is a lady with a rolling suitcase.
To her right is a young boy on a bicycle.

With natural grace and instinctive fear,
the doe ambles back down the slope to shelter.
Across the street at a bus stop, I realized
I had no idea how to provide help or comfort.

Not long before I was born, wild animals
roamed free throughout this part of town.
The street immediately north of the one
on which I live is called Huntingwood.

In the high rise aspiration
for hastily erected concrete and glass
amidst the cacophony of constant traffic
the presence of a deer seems out of place.

# North

Oh Canada I love thee
I will always stand on guard for you.
But until it's free for EVERYONE
it cannot be strong or true.

# The Day After Canada Day

Riding the Via Train to Kingston
the one-time capital of Canada
to read at my favourite poetry festival.

About three hours north of Kingston
a "Convoy" of protestors have invaded Ottawa
seeking a very personal version of freedom.

We are living in times where many feel
their rights have been stolen from them
and that they must fight for their entitlement.

This seems like a surreal distraction
from a reality where more and more people
have to decide between rent and dinner.

It would be very easy for me to push
the recline button on the arm of the train seat
and just for a couple of days

let the world's troubles pass by unrecognized
like the out of focus landscape
rolling outside the window.

But the blessings of a weekend excursion
are not enough to make me give up hope
for the Canada in which I believe.

# Simcoe Day
*for James Deahl*

About 30 minutes before sunset
you go outside to scoop and shovel
the remnants of the previous evening
from your Muskoka fireplace.

Just as you did the night before
you make a bed of yellow birch bark
dried red maple leaves, balsam fir needles
and toilet paper rolls in the centre of the pit.

Then, you make a tepee around this base -
branches of maple treated in resin from the fir.
You take pride in the geometric precision
of your creation as you set it ablaze.

This evening is a celebration in honour
of an underappreciated long weekend
often referred to as Civic Holiday
on calendars and paystub summaries.

There is a hint of autumn in the wind
and your fireplace is dug into a hill
so the flame does not immediately catch
and you have to repeat the steps of your labours.

The other party-goers, interlopers
into your preferred evening calm
all give their opinions of what is wrong
with everything you are trying to do.

They audibly gasp
as you return from under the deck

with four logs of weeping willow
and put one of them in the fireplace.

And don't they all give you
the full value of their expertise, proclaiming
willow needs to season at least a full year
before you tell them you cut it last August.

Still, you like these people, and you share
the warmth you prepared for this evening.
But they are unable to appreciate it
to the extent which you can.

Because you are the one who took the saw to the trees
you are the one who used an axe to form the pieces
you are the one who coated them all in resin
and you are the one who dug the firepit.

# Poutine

I love Poutine!

Real Canadian Poutine, that is.

Cubes of cheddar cheese deliberately curdled, mixed with the fatty drippings of well cooked meat, poured on a massive bed of French fried potatoes.

What could possibly be wrong with that?

My friend Norman took me to Chez Claudette on rue Laurier in Montreal. I had the Elvis, with ground beef, onions, and assorted peppers. It was incredible. An extremely satisfying meal! I experienced none of the lethargy I usually do after eating fast food. I felt like I had just eaten the best, healthiest dinner of my life.

I love real Canadian Poutine.

Unlike the other kind, which is vile and unwholesome and abominable and a sin against creation and trying to take over Eastern Europe.

# #RAPTORS

The pride of our nation
one team we all root for
and stand by through thick and thin
if you truly love the Raptors.

Soul
a unifying force
no black or yellow or white
just one love which binds us together
at least for two hours and fifteen minutes.

Mind expands
takes in the grandeur
of such collaboration
of the quest for greatness
and a fun Friday night.

We are a body rising as one
on cue to sing "O Canada"
cheer for Pascal and Scottie B
and OG and Fred Van Vleet
and boo the referee.

This scene is not for those
who are here to be seen
but are here to watch
these elite athletes
do their best for each other and for us.

So let's truly love the Raptors
and stand by them through thick and thin.
One team we all root for
the pride of our nation.

# Advent

My three-legged slow-footed exit from work
not having made a single dollar that day
despite thirty minutes overtime.

Three elevators are packed with strangers I
see every day, their public faces under dull eyes
on the brink of feeling. I get on the fourth elevator.

The bus seats are dotted with those wearing masks.
Those not wearing masks bear oversized bags filled
with holiday gifts and what might be pride or despair.

Darkness has fallen on the city.
The flickering lights and honking horns
of frozen traffic create a cacophonous nightmare.

On Saturday morning I wake up
glad I don't have to go to work
until I remember I have to go shopping.

To try and tell the people I love
            how much I love them
even though I have no idea what to buy.

But at least I have people to love
enough to go to a crowded mall on my day off.
With a sigh of resignation, I get out of bed.

I open the blinds and look out the window
watch squirrels climb the cold, leafless trees
and somehow know something great is coming.

# Scars

I have scars on my knees.

They look like smiley-faces, depending upon your perspective.

Or, they may look like a thoughtful frown, a reminder of unhappier days, try-
 ing in vain to be
a hockey star, instead of being satisfied with being merely good.

But, this was only one reason why I was unhappy.

We didn't call it depression in those days. Certainly, guys wouldn't have called
 it that, at least
not hockey guys.

I rarely wear shorts because I don't want anybody to see the scars on my knees.

There are other scars no one can define, no matter the length of my trousers.

However, they are ironically the hardest ones to hide.

# Kingston Road in the 1980's

Three slices of moist bread cut diagonally
layers of bacon, lettuce, and tomato –
this is when they put mayonnaise
on a BLT, or at least Miracle Whip.

French fries scooped out of a plastic tub,
always cooked a little less or a little more
than you would have preferred, topped
with pepper and salt and saltier gravy.

A can of lukewarm Coca Cola foaming
over the rim of a parfait glass filled
with so much ice it took at least
three pours to drink it all.

Or a cup of coffee, the third one of the day–
the equalizer, the source of fake energy–
which sat in the pot for over two hours,
and needed three teaspoons of sugar.

Mini jukeboxes within an arms length
asked only for the quarters you didn't spend
at the video arcade, so you could play a song
and tell your friend it was your favourite.

# Again
## *1986*

it's just as well

I did not intend
to sit and shiver

in an oversized
orange garbage bag

with a greasy lip
and watch them lose

Again

# Wire
## *(TRHA)*

My nerves are wound like piano wire
wrapped around my wrists and ankles
etched into my face and bleeding heart
while I scream into a vacuum.

Forgetting the madness I left behind
I remember our sacred, smelly hill
where we used to smoke and talk
about when things would be different.

We cut through barbed wire. The fangs
which sank inside and tried to tear
us apart, we overcame, until all that
remained was what bound us together.

# Juice

The salesmen in their ill-fitting suits
shuffle their feet in a rhythmless dance
around the coffee machine, try not to look
each other in the eye as they mumble,
"Good morning", beneath the stereo
blaring, "Everyone's a Winner".

Then, the Hugo Boss wearing manager
enters, followed by an aura of Polo
stronger than the dimple in his chin,
lowers the volume on the stereo,
turns to the salesmen and asks,
"How is everyone feeling today?"

"Fantastic, terrific, oh yeah strong,
juice baby sucker, I feel wonderful
right on, right on, right on,
juice, juice, juice, juice!"

# Center

I walk streets of unfulfilled promise
in quest of a passage to fortune
defined by a measure of success
which cannot last.

I hold on to solitary pleasures
which only fulfill the need
to seek out such emptiness.

Deep within I feel a spark
and try to let it burn through the gloom.

This spark becomes a voice who says:
"You are the only one to blame
if you give up your dream."

I cry out defiance, it's not my fault,
my dream has been taken from me.
The salt of my tears becomes bitter
as I try to wipe away my shame.

"Don't be afraid
to believe in your dream.
As soon as you do it becomes real!

"Then let it go, and it will grow
into something greater than you could imagine."

# Spiritual Warfare
*Growth and Change*


On the journey
we all go on
but not together

the inner battle
defines the outer man;
we cannot avoid the truth.

Whatever God or
notion of the Divine
one holds as Holy

each seeks the sacred
absolute oneness
with the absolute

the best that we can be
and that which is beyond
the best that we can comprehend.

What holds me back
is not real, and yet:
Far more real than reality.

The it which strikes the itch
I cannot help but scratch
leaves me bitter, bloody, and raw.

But better to be on the barbed-wire path
to meet and struggle with anguish
than to live a living death.

O Master whom I always seek
in my hope and in despair
please rest and bless my spirit.

# In My Own Words

To have the story told
clearly and sincerely
with no pretension.

Beckoning all who might listen
with an open heart and
a sense of humour

because I want you
to hear my message
but also enjoy how it's said.

I'm not naïve. I know
we live in an imperfect world
but I believe in ultimate good.

I desire a community of peace,
love and unity, where we all
can aspire to our dreams.

When I meet someone
who shares this belief with me
I see things already getting better.

# The Real Stuff

No happy endings
No altruisms
No pain I don't want to feel
By myself

Late-night tip-tapping
On my type-writer
Old-school notions
Change your mind
By my words

The nights get later
The words don't get deeper
I need more time
To get ready
So I say...

By day
I bring cough drops of peace
And comfort, for the man,
Who said to the Cinderella Man,
"You can break his ribs, you can do it!"

The world comes
Anon to get certified
Allowed to have
A similar conversation
In fifteen other languages

Glad that I, with all my experience,
Don't have to compete
For hours...

I'm waiting for the basis,
Of what I am to start,
To make my life begin

Or, at least, to be in the flow;
Which defines me as a poet

# Middle-Aged White Men Are Ruining the World

The Saturday bus ride to Morningside is so much better
than my weekday drudgery along Sheppard
up whichever connecting route presents itself
to get me east on Finch to my workplace.

Everybody is in a better mood, more courteous
more concerned about others around them.
They are on their way to fun excursions, or shopping
to meet their needs, as well as those of whom they love.

The Morningside bus ride south is even better. The bus takes
longer to arrive, but the driver wants to chat and be part
of the community, part of your day. Everyone makes room
for baby carriages and people with canes and each other.

But not LAST Saturday.

A guy about my age got on the Morningside bus with his two sons.
Two stops later, a kind enough looking guy, clearly down
on his luck, maybe hadn't eaten in a while, entreats
the driver to let him on the bus without paying.

The guy about my age turns to his sons, shakes his head,
saying, "The driver let him on the bus for free."
The two sons were at that age where their view
of the entire universe was filtered through their father.

What an entitled, arrogant, self-righteous, ignorant...
What kind of legacy are we leaving behind?
What kind of world are we leaving for the children?
What else can we teach them other than right or wrong?

I wondered how he would feel in the unlikely event
either he or one of his sons were in that predicament.

# All I Could Get Down
*for S.O'B*


I wanted to write a poem.

It was going to be witty, clever, and have lasting social significance.

The sort of thing that might get me noticed, and hopefully printed in a grass-roots literary journal.

My intention was to create something that would make your day better, if not change the world.

Because I believe in the power of poetry.

I was attaining to the heights I can only find in pure language and the quest for truth.

Since you are still reading, I assume these images resonate with you.

Please come inside.

I apologize for the mess.

It is the result of uncontrolled impulse, blood pressure raised by the pursuit of nothingness, conflict without resolution, and the other false notions which pass for thought.

Still, I have my training to fall back on. Many layers of the multi-disciplinary false appeal to authority I founded my adolescence and young adulthood on ignoring.

If I unwound and rewove even one thread from this convoluted tapestry, I would have the slack to create something worth binding.

But I just ran out of beer.

# The Path
### *with a line or two borrowed from Frost*

Two roads diverged in the verdant woods—
I have taken them both.

By God's Grace, He has allowed me to make
many mistakes, have foolish adventures

experiences pleasurable and pointless—
but I survived them all, apparently.

Just before I slid into the slimy bog
made by my own crapulence

He pulled me out, and put me on the path
which had been waiting for me all along.

Sometimes, I still drift off to the side
distracted by memories of darkness.

I embrace a sense of emptiness, instead
of experiencing fear and uncertainty.

It seems comfortable being in despair
the state I once accepted as my destiny

when I can't see by the light through
the trees the end I hope and long for.

Then, I hear a soft voice from deep within
asking me to return. And I heed the call.

The journey has become everything to me.
And that has made all the difference.

# Big Time
## *Local Player Makes Good*

First round lottery pick
signed to a guaranteed contract
it seems he has fulfilled
the stuff of little-boy dreams.

Even as a raw upstart
clickety-clacking on coltish legs
he showed signs this day might come
if ever he grew into his promise.

He watched how the game
was being played and decided
to learn how to do it a different way
and work as long as it took to seem simple.

He never forgot where he came from.
"I owe it all to my family, my coaches,
my teammates, and even my opponents,
because they forced me to be better."

I asked him how he would celebrate
having found what he was looking for.
With a glint in his eye, he set his jaw,
and said, "I've only just begun."

# What I Do for a Living

I sell
Japanese-inspired
Chinese-manufactured

German engineered
Malaysian-printed
Honduran-designed

American-owned
Canadian distributed
no one knows what it's for.

# Try

the world tries
to tell me
I am something
I am not
and I fight back
and I lose
so I try
to be what they say
they want me to be
and I succeed on their terms
for a moment
and then the moment passes
so I try
to be myself again
and I fail
and then I try
something different
and I fail
but the failure
seems to be
the shit I must get through
so I can
finally grow up
so I laugh
not a maniacal laugh
merely a buffer
against the underlying darkness
which tries
to overwhelm me
but
I rise
try to clean myself up
and realize

this is the day
I become
a little more
human

# Lead with Love

*"The world is burning; now is not the time to be talking of unimportant things."* — St. Teresa of Avila

The smoky haze of the sunless dawn
burns my eyes and throat and
tastes like a barbecue gone bad,
so I imagine this is what hell is like.

I am going where I have to go. The smoke
follows like the memory of a nightmare,
gets into my clothes, gets into my lungs,
until I am a coughing, wheezing mess.

No one says, "Hello, how are you?"
They order lunch with rice and MSG
to remind me that I don't belong –
but I will lead with love.

The rejection I encounter,
is really fear of the machine,
of not being absorbed into a lie,
and the worst part is the indifference.

When everything means nothing,
and the light I seek cannot be seen,
and hope is hidden deep inside,
I can still lead with love.

# Country Road
## *for Andrew*

*"It is with the smallest brushes that the artist paints
the most exquisitely beautiful pictures." — Brother André*

The air is cold, but not as cold
as it would usually be in January.
You are dressed for the journey:
jacket, touque, gloves, and boots.
The dirt road is not wet or icy,
but made uneven by tire tracks,
so you have to watch your step.

The tire tracks are not fresh
and there are no cars on the road.
There are no people, no animals–
even your cell phone is quiet.
You learn to accept the silence,
feel your breath expand your lungs,
and fully connect with the moment.

About half a kilometre ahead,
two clusters of leafless trees,
one on either side of the road,
seem to rise from patches of snow.
A mist blurs the trees like a dream
and covers what lies beyond them.
But you keep walking.

# Down Time

She turned the key to her apartment door.
She wished this was the end of her day,
a chance to put on sweats and collapse.
But she only had enough of a break
to make dinner for her children.

She took time to say hello, what are you
watching on TV, is your homework done?
She processed the mail, mostly bills, as well as
answering machine messages offering extra shifts
she couldn't take because she already had to work.

In the refrigerator she found butter, orange juice
and a wilted head of lettuce. In the cupboard was
one lonely can of beef stew. She would have to find
something to eat at her overnight job, and go to the
food bank in the morning when she would usually sleep.

Her son tugged at her pant leg. She softly said she was
getting his dinner ready before she went back to work.
He cried and begged her to stay. Her daughter used
a hockey stick to slap a tennis ball against the bare wall
where her grandmother's china cabinet used to be.

"Would you both please stop?", she asked. But her son
cried more and her daughter's slapshots got louder.
As the stew was about to start simmering, the power
went out. She slammed the spatula against the stove,
"I didn't graduate from university to end up like this!"

# Pantoum

The smouldering fire of his heart
stoked by hope borne of a long wait
was yet truly the very start
of uncovering such a trait.

Stoked by hope borne of a long wait
he learns the truth within the dream
of uncovering such a trait
beauty greater than what may seem.

He learns the truth within the dream
the radiant light in his eyes
beauty greater than what may seem
coaxing his desire to arise.

The radiant light in his eyes
was yet truly the very start
coaxing his desire to arise
the smouldering fire of his heart.

# Trust
## Inspired by the U2 song "40"

I've spent years in the wilderness
in the desert of my despair
so I may learn to trust and
believe it will get better.

I trod the grapes in the
winepress of my affliction.
I try in vain to slake
my thirst on the overflow.

I wrestle with nameless fears
wallow in deep misery
while the devil's angels prey
upon my weakness.

Since my sins and fears cannot
be offered up as a substitute
for this journey, I will accept
the grace beyond my understanding.

I waited patiently for the Lord
He inclined and heard my cry
He brought me up out of the pit
Out of the mire and clay

I will sing, sing a new song
I will sing, sing a new song

# Darkness

I am a child of the light
who has known the deepest darkness.

I am tempted and tortured
by the very pain you are
except in a different way.

It comes into my house, my heart
but only after I accept it.
I foolishly think I can change
darkness into light on my own.

When I let the darkness into my home
it burrows into my soul, my sacred fire
my deepest creativity, my passion
my reason, and my reason for living.

No matter how I try, I
cannot change the darkness.
The darkness consumes me
when I give in to doubt.

The darkness tells me
everything I believe in is a lie
there is no purpose in this world
nothing worth living or dying for.

The darkness tells me
there is no love, only hatred.
Everyone I know wants to hurt me
and I should hurt them before they can.

I drink a lot of beer from time to time,
swear like a sailor when I am sober,
eat salt and vinegar potato chips, and
love my local sports teams a little too much.

But I will never give in to the darkness.

# A Matter of Faith

*"What strength do I have left, that I should wait [and hope]?*
*And what is ahead of me, that I should be patient and endure?"*
*— Job 6:11 (AMPC)*

The world resumes their never-ending wars
without a plan for peaceful resolution.

And our city is a bastion of the entitled, who
use othering as their cause and their weapon.

Compared to those in the line of fire,
you realize how little your problems are,
even though you are overwhelmed by them.

But what if the battle is being waged
by forces beyond what you can see?

Long-suffering is when such forces strive
to kill the light, and you choose to stand firm.

This is the struggle to overcome despair!
It requires inner strength and infinite joy,
and faith in the glory of the light.

# Micah

I see Micah at first light
by the road where I must go
rocking on his broad oak chair
he nods and bids me, "Good day."

I shake my head as I pass
wonder why he isn't still in his bed
if he doesn't have to face the morning
the way every honest man should.

I struggle with my labours
to conform to my surroundings
so I might earn or be made worthy
of a pleasant journey through this life.

I meet Micah sitting on his porch
as I take the winding road home.
I ask if he might like to spare
a glass of wine to ease my pain.

He laughs, he cries,
"Please be here tomorrow
about the same time and I will
share something much sweeter!"

I guess whatever he has for me
will keep until the chosen time.
I am left with a sense of possibility -
something to ponder until I get there.

When I return around the bend
to keep our appointment, I expect
he has forgotten. But he is standing
in front of his chair, and bids me welcome.

He hands me a cup of cold water
which settles into me quite well.
"I know what you are looking for,"
he says, "and it is all I have to offer.

"You see me sit here every day
and I see you shake your head.
You see me staring at the sky
and question what I live for.

"Hope. Unshakeable, unbreakable hope.
Not wishful thinking, or an easier path.
Not riches nor the respect of your fellow man.
But the reason, the purpose to see it through.

"My back is not strong enough for heavy labour
my stomach isn't strong enough for commerce
so there is little for me to do in this world
except wait for a better one to appear.

"I have neither position nor possessions
nothing to mark or make my remembrance.
So, I will hold on as long as it takes
for something greater to come over the horizon.

# Ecumenism
*for Hal Clark, Jr.*

In a church not of my
original denomination
Pastor Steve gave the
Word of Life to 4 people
as if we were four hundred.

One day at work, Kash Ali saw
I was having a bad day chasing
fantasies, and reminded me the
most important thing is family –
and that we all are one.

The sacraments and rituals
we learn are a necessary blessing.
But the direction where they lead
the only judgment I will abide
is that God loves us.

# The Day of my Dad's Memorial
## 2 Cor 5: 1-9, 15-17

Fog rolled over
the Douglas Fir lined hills
all the way to the St. John's Regatta.

The Regatta was a day late this year
due to wind and rain which never came
and yet pushed back the Civic Holiday.

"Old Man" by Neil Young played
on the oldies station. I hope I'm not
too much like my old man was.

When my Dad passed away,
we hadn't had a real conversation
in over 10 years, or seen each other in fifteen.

I walked with Cousin David and Linda
through the Anglican cemetery to reach
the shores of Quidi Vidi Lake.

They shook hands and embraced everyone
they knew and even those few they didn't.
It was their first live race in three years.

Perfect strangers nodded and smiled
and said hello as they passed by. I let go
of the Toronto in me to return the greeting.

We passed by dozens of food trucks, and I
was struck by three in a well spaced U-shape
called Ziggy Peelgood's Famous Fries.

David said, "You have to try Ziggy's,
and there will be a lineup at lunchtime.
But anything worth having is worth the wait."

This was the first year that women rowed
full course races. Women have always been
strong enough to carry us, but it's something.

Our vantage point allowed us to see perhaps
a quarter of the race, providing just enough
opportunity to root for those falling behind.

In my memories of St. John's in August, I
usually wore a heavy sweater. But, on this day,
my golf shirt was stuck to my skin.

During a lull between races, the wind began
to move like a blessing, and Linda said,
"I think we might have a bit of rain."

I prayed for rain, rain to make the forest fire
go out, rain to clean the foul sweat off me,
rain to prepare for what comes next.

At 4:00, David turned left off Topsail Road
into Holy Sepulchre Cemetery, to visit my Dad's
ashes interred above the patriarchal plot.

My Dad was the youngest of twelve.
Some of the cousins joined to pay tribute.
Along with Linda, David, and me,

there were Brian and Evangeline
Gerry and Geraldine, and I will
always be grateful for their support.

I read parts of 2nd Corinthians
Chapter 5, and said Amen, and after a
moment of silence, we went and had a time.

I got to Newfoundland
too late to make peace with my Dad.
But, I am finally at peace with myself.

# After Four of Us Have Been Let Go
## for Angela

*And all is seared with trade; bleared, smeared with toil;*

from "God's Grandeur", Gerard Manley Hopkins

We tip-toe through the office
try not to be seen or breathe too loud,
overcome by a sense of, not quite surprise—
we knew this could be your reaction
when costs are up and profits are down
and the people we call don't want to buy
*tchotchkes** since they can't pay their bills
and had to fire their own people.

We don't know how to feel.
Should we be relieved it wasn't us
or afraid that we will be next?
Should we be sad our friends have lost
their livelihood and don't know where
they will end up, or glad they don't
have to go through life hating themselves
so you can make another dollar?

We know you like money.
We need it, too. We use it to pay
for our homes and feed our kids
and get to the office so we can
make you some more money.
But we are also living, breathing
human beings with hopes and
dreams beyond your bottom line.

---

* *tchotchkes* (Yiddish) are trinkets which are more decorative than functional

You need us.
You need us to sell your stuff,
and do it with skill and personality.
We need you.
We need you to value our work
and treat us with respect and dignity.

# Supper

Through the crisp ruddy twilight
fingers and arms entwined, we enter
my newfound favourite sushi spot
toward the end of the Village.

She lets go of my hand, twirls
almost perfectly around the table
on which I manage to keep balance -
she smiles as we sit in our chairs.

She asks me how my day has gone
where else I could be this evening.
I tell her everything I have ever
hoped for is right across from me.

Our server comes over, wonders
what we would like to start. She
orders a glass of white wine. I
get ice water and ginger ale.

She says, "Honey, if you want to have
a beer, it's okay." I reply, "Thank
you for your kind indulgence. But
I am sure I indulged enough last night."

I am glad she chooses to be with me
when clearly she could do better.
She has seen me at my worst
and not just in a lampshade.

I know she fell in love with my
second best, but living what
the years have brought, I am
finally ready to give her more.

We share tempura, sushi roll and sashimi
she deftly lifts on poplar chopsticks.
I spear too much wasabi with my fork
then practically inhale the pickled ginger.

I wipe tears from my eyes, then look into hers.
What we have is greater than who we are.
I know there is no getting out
and I don't want to be let go.

# Acknowledgments

I am very grateful to Howard Aster and Michael Walsh of Mosaic Press for supporting and publishing my work, and to my friend and mentor Terry Barker, without whom none of this would have happened.

# Some Notes on Prior Publication

**"The Long Defeat that Brings Us What We Know"** *Agape Review*, July 2021; Poetry Present, September 3rd, 2022. Also, as with a number of these poems, they appeared in *Worth the Wait*, published by Cactus Press in April, 2023.

**"Becoming"** Tending the Fire, League of Canadian Poets, May 2020; *Lummox Anthology #9*, November 2020; *The Celebration of Poetry 20th Anniversary Anthology*, Beret Days Press, March 2021; *The Literary Parrot Anthology*, July 2021; Consonant Light, IOWI, July 2022; Poetry Pause, August 2nd, 2022; *Prodigy Magazine*, August 2022.

**"Prisoner"** Poetry Present, October 16, 2021; *Hunger: An Anthology*, Transcendent Zero Press, January 2022; BeZine blog, April 10, 2022; DarkWinterLit.com, May 30th, 2022.

**"Toil"** *Literature for the People*, Issue 2, April 2021; *Morning Muse*, Issue 4/5, October 2022; Envoy #121, November 2022; *Rabble Review* No. 6, April 2023.

**"Hemispheres"** *Poetry in the Plague Year* online Anthology, August 2020; *WordCity Monthly*, Issue 6, February 2021.

**"Moments in Time"** *Quarantine Review, Holiday Special*, December 31, 2020.

**"The New Normal"** *Harbinger Asylum*, Spring 2021.

**"Our Road"** *CP Quarterly*, Issue 12, Spring 2021; *Morning Muse*, Autumn 2021; *Otherwise Engaged Literature and Arts Journal*, Volume 11, July 2023; *Envoy 123*, July 2023.

**"Virus"** *Canadian Stories*, October/November 2020; *WordCity Monthly*, Issue 14, March 2022.

**"Vacation"** Canadian Stories, August/September 2021; *WordCity Monthly*, Issue 14, March 2022.

**"Aphorisms of the CoronApocalypse"** *Poetry and Covid*, December 2020; *Consonant Light*, July 2022; *Prodigy Magazine*, August 2022; *People's Voice*, December 2022.

**"Voices"** *The People's Voice*, July 1–31, 2021.

**"The World is On Fire"** Reckonings and Reconciliation exhibition at Lawrence House Centre for the Arts, October 2021; *Qutub Minar Review*, April 2022; *BeZine*, Spring 2023.

**"Hope"** *Northern Voices Journal,* March 2013; Litterateur, March 2021; *Spirit Fire Review,* December 2022.

**"Eternal"** Poems for Ephesians, McMaster Divinity College website, December 16th, 2020; *The Poet Magazine,* Faith issue, April 2021.

**"Violet"** *Agape Review,* December 2021; *Morning Muse,* Winter 2022; *Spirit Fire Review,* December 2022.

**"New"** *In Silence We Wait,* Hidden Brook Press, February 2021; *WordCity Monthly,* Issue 14, March 2022.

**"Ode to My Dad"** *Canadian Stories,* June/July 2022.

**"Finding Myself"** *BeZine blog,* April 10, 2022; *Canadian Stories Magazine,* June/July 2022; *Envoy 123,* July 2023.

**"Bad Poem About Aging"** *Canadian Stories,* February/March 2023.

**"Good Brains"** *Canadian Stories,* October/November 2020.

**"Aspire"** *Agape Review,* October 2021.

**"All I Have to Do is Write"** *Envoy 121,* November 2022.

**"Calling"** *Envoy 123,* July 2023.

**"Out of My Own Words"** *Haiku zbornik Ludbreg* 2021, August; *Here and Now,* September 2022.

**"Alone"** and **"Burning Summer"** were also in *Here and Now.*

**"Apocalypse Not"** *Devour,* Issue 9, September 2020.

**"The Day Before Canada Day"** *Canadian Stories,* October/November 2022; *Poetry Pause,* July 14 2023.

**"North"** *Canadian Stories,* October/November 2022.

**"The Day After Canada Day"** *Canadian Stories,* October/November 2022; *Rabble Review* No. 5, January 2023.

**"Simcoe Day"** *Canadian Stories,* June/July 2020.

**"Poutine"** *Canadian Stories,* February/March 2023.

**"#Raptors"** *Toronto Poetry Magazine,* September 2022.

**"Scars"** *Front Lines: Bent Not Broken,* TWC Press, 2020; *Morning Muse,* Winter 2022.

**"Kingston Road in the 1980's"** *Devour,* Winter 2022–23; Poetry Pause, September 5th, 2023 (pending).

**"Again"** *Canadian Stories,* August/September 2021.

**"Wire"** *New York Parrot,* June 28, 2021; *Morning Muse,* Winter 2022.

**"Juice"** Lothlorien Poetry Journal Blog, March 2023; Volume 21, April 2023.

**"Center"** *Qutub Minar Review,* April 2022; *Canadian Stories Magazine,* June/July 2022.

**"Spiritual Warfare"** *The Wordsmith Journal Magazine,* September 2013; *The Poet Magazine,* Faith Issue, April 2021.

**"In My Own Words"** Big Art Book 2014, May 2014; *Cooch Behar Patrik*, Issue 1, August 2021. Another version of it was also part of an anthology called *Bottom of the Wine Jar*, published by SandCrab Press in 2017.

**"The Real Stuff"** Envoy Newsletter, April 2016; *Aquillrelle Magazine*, May 2016.

**"Middle-Aged White Men are Ruining the World"** *Canadian Stories*, June/July 2020; BeZine blog, April 10, 2022.

**"All I Could Get Down"** *Canadian Stories*, August/September 2021; *Envoy 121*, November 2022.

**"The Path"** *Front Lines: Until the Words Run Pure*, TWC Press, 2020; *The Poet Magazine*, Faith Issue, Spring 2021; *Consonant Light*, July 2022.

**"Big Time"** *WordCity Monthly*, Issue 6, February 2021.

**"What I Do for a Living"** *Envoy 108*, March 2021; *Morning Muse* Issue 4/5, October 2022; *Jasper's Folly Poetry Journal*, Issue 1, January 2023.

**"Try"** *Brave World Magazine*, Vol. 3, March 2021; *Cooch Behar Anthology*, February, 2022; BeZine blog, April 10, 2022.

**"Country Road"** *Over the Garden Fence*, February 2023.

**"Down Time"** *Rabble Review* No. 5, January 2023.

**"Pantoum"** *Canadian Stories*, June/July 2020; Lummox 9 Anthology, November 2020; *WordCity Monthly*, Issue 6, February 2021; *Envoy 117*, December 2021; *Consonant Light*, July 2022.

**"Darkness"** *Canadian Stories*, February/March 2023 (featured poem).

**"Micah"** *Literature for the People*, issue 2, April 2021; *Consonant Light*, July 2022; *Prodigy Magazine*, August 2022.

**"Ecumenism"** *Agape Review*, May 29, 2022.

**"The Day of My Dad's Memorial"** *Agape Review*, January 2023.

**"Supper"** Beliveau Review, issue 4, Spring 2021.

# Praise for *The Long Defeat*

"His poems don't embellish reality; they don't attempt to smooth the edges. They resonate with the reader precisely because they find life's pain points and have the courage to gaze directly into that pain. The more profound the appeal to higher wisdom, to true goodness, to God. In his texts, there is the tremulous breath of life."

— **Vita Shtivelman**
poet, translator, and founder of
Club EtCetera

"Patrick Connors is a poet's poet who speaks as one who has been there as he takes us along on a memory-guided emotion-filled journey."

— **PJ Yukon**
Yukon Poet Laureate

*The Long Defeat* is a prayer for humanity. Out of the wellspring of his faith and personal suffering, Patrick Connors leads with love and hope towards a better world."

— **Jennifer Hosein**
author and visual artist

"The poems in *The Long Defeat* affirm the right to strive, whether against personal disappointment or the difficult challenges of our age: the pandemic, injustice, environmental degradation. But they also affirm the discovery of beauty in unlikely places, the power of poetry, the importance of integrity and poetic growth. These modest, honest, unswerving poems draw the reader past defeat into resolve and renewal."

— **Elizabeth Greene**
author of *A Season Among Psychics*
and *Understories*

"Artfully varied in form, tone, and subject, and not without occasional humour and satirical bite, their observant concerns and introspections admit frailty, missteps, and self-doubt. They do not preach, whine or scold but testify frankly and unpretentiously to the challenges of lifelong spiritual navigation. Ultimately, they speak a refusal to be overcome, with the aim instead to refresh and uplift: affirming the triune bedrock of faith, hope, and love."

—**Allan Briesmaster**
author of *The Long Bond* and *Windfor*

"These are prayerful, sometimes declamatory poems that aim for light, love, and hope amid dark times ... of pandemic worries and in the general tumult of our strife-filled world. As you read, you may alternate between laughing and becoming teary-eyed. Honesty, thoughtfulness, and straightforwardness are Connors' calling cards in this worthwhile collection."

— **Meg Freer**
author of *Serve the Sorrowing World with Joy* and
*A Man of Integrity*

"Patrick leads the reader through life excavations, the anxiety of the early pandemic, and the moments of social justice that brought deep humility and transformation. With accessible narrative style, this book holds a power and humble path for growth and personal change."

— **Charlie Petch**
Winter of the 2022 ReLit Award for Poetry

"The always reflective verse of Patrick Connors shimmers again with humility and humanity in his new collection *The Long Defeat*. Few contemporary poets strive the way Connors does. His poems are so ardent and unadorned in their plea for a better world and a better self, that they will disarm any reader's pretensions."

— **Devon Gallant**
author of five books of poetry, founder of Cactus Press
and the host of Accent, a Montreal-based literary reading series

"*The Long Defeat* is an intimate gaze into a compassionate poet's heart during one of the darkest points of our collective history. It asks questions without simple answers: *what does it mean to be alive in a time of precarity? How does one confront a sense of self in the face of death? How does the drone of day-to-day existence birth the possibility of an unforeseeable future?* ... Brimming with resonant imagery and confessions of wonder and loss, *The Long Defeat* is an invitation to find grace in the act of living itself."

— **Sheniz Janmohamed**
author and artist educator